PLAYBACK+

Speed • Pitch • Balance • Loop

To access audio visit:
www.halleonard.com/mylibrary

"Enter Code"
3574-1976-3707-0039

ISBN 978-1-59615-637-1

Music Minus One

EXCLUSIVELY DISTRIBUTED BY

HAL•LEONARD®

Visit Hal Leonard Online at
www.halleonard.com

Contact Us:
Hal Leonard
7777 West Bluemound Road
Milwaukee, WI 53213
Email: info@halleonard.com

In Europe contact:
Hal Leonard Europe Limited
42 Wigmore Street
Marylebone, London, W1U 2RN
Email: info@halleonardeurope.com

In Australia contact:
Hal Leonard Australia Pty. Ltd.
4 Lentara Court
Cheltenham, Victoria, 3192 Australia
Email: info@halleonard.com.au

Contents

HOW TO USE THIS BOOK/AUDIO

This package provides:

1. Basic instruction on how to play bluegrass banjo, with banjo tablature for thirteen solos.

2. An opportunity to play along with a full bluegrass band under normal playing conditions. In general, the banjo has a backup role, with one or two spaces for soloing in each song.

The music is recorded with the banjo by itself in the right channel, and the rest of the band, including vocals, in the left channel. The banjo's volume is balanced with the rest of the band: sometimes loud, sometimes barely audible, depending on what is appropriate. To hear the banjo, more clearly, you can adjust the balance using the *PlayBack+* feature online. A separate track is provided when you wish to play along. For songs that start with the banjo, there is a count-off that indicates when to begin. If you follow the count, the rest of the band will come in with you right in time.

If you're a beginner, I strongly suggest getting an instruction book and/or lessons if possible, for a stronger foundation.

Whenever you pick up your banjo, the first thing you should do is tune up. On the first audio track, I've recorded the correct pitch for each of the five strings on a banjo. Adjust the tuning peg for each string until it matches the pitch on the recording. Start with the first string (high D), the one closest to the floor when the banjo is in playing position. Work your way up to the fifth string (high G), the one with the peg halfway up the neck. If each string is in tune, strumming all five strings together gives a nice-sounding G chord.

The next step is to acquaint yourself with the main chord formations used in bluegrass:

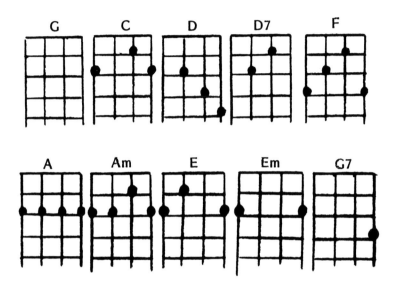

Practice G, C, and D7 until you can switch between them quickly and accurately, preferably without looking. Make sure your fingers are just behind the correct frets. To check accuracy, play each string of the chord and make sure each note is clear.

Try strumming chords while you sing the songs on the following pages.

THE BALLAD OF JED CLAMPETT

by Paul Henning
KEY: G
CAPO: OFF

*play a C# chord
by moving a C
up one fret

```
       G                      Am       D
Come and listen to my story bout a man named Jed
                                    G
Poor mountaineer, barely kept his family fed.
                          C          C#*
Then one day he was shootin' at some food, and
D                             G
Up through the ground came a bubbling crude. . .
```

(Oil, that is. . . black gold. . . Texas tea. . .)

FOGGY MOUNTAIN BREAKDOWN

by Earl Scruggs
KEY: G
CAPO: OFF

See chords page 9.

IT'S IN MY MIND TO RAMBLE

by Peter Wernick
KEY: G
CAPO: OFF

```
   G         F          G
It's been quite a while since I've seen you my dear,
       D            G
I've been gone a long long time.
                       F              G
All those nights on the road I've been talking to myself
 D                      G
I can't believe I left you behind.
```

(Chorus)
```
It's in my mind to ramble, I hope you'll understand
                   F        G
Sometimes I find I just have to go.
 C                           G
I know it's hard my darling, forgive me if you can,
                 D       G
Cause you know that I love you so.
```


SALTY DOG BLUES

(public domain)
KEY ON RECORD: A
CAPO: 2ND FRET

```
G                               E
Standing on the corner with the lowdown blues,
A
Great big hole in the bottom of my shoes,
D                          G
Honey let me be your salty dog.
                    E
Let me be your salty dog
 A
Or I won't be your little man at all,
D                          G
Honey let me be your salty dog.
```


DARK HOLLOW

(public domain)
KEY ON RECORD: E
CAPO: 2ND FRET

No banjo break.
```
       D    A      D
I'd rather be in some dark hollow
            G    D
Where the sun refuse to shine
              D7   G
Than to be here alone, knowing that you're gone,
         D      A     D
It would cause me to lose my mind.
         [same chords for chorus]
```


LATE LAST NIGHT

(public domain)
KEY ON RECORD: A
CAPO: 2ND FRET

```
        C               G
It was late last night when Willie came home
D                 G
Heard him a-knocking on the door
C                          G
Slipping and a-sliding with his new shoes on
           D              G
Papa said Willie, don't you rap no more..
         [same chords for chorus]
```


DUELING BANJOS

(public domain)
KEY: A
CAPO: 2ND FRET

MOUNTAIN DEW
(public domain)
KEY ON RECORD: A
CAPO: 2ND FRET

G
My uncle Mort, he's sawed off and short,
   C   G
He measures about four foot two

But he thinks he's a giant when you give him a pint
                   D   G
Of that good old mountain dew.
  [same chords for chorus]

LONESOME ROAD BLUES
(public domain)
KEY ON RECORD: B
CAPO: 4TH FRET

    G
I'm going down that long lonesome road, Lord Lord,
   C   G
I'm going down that long lonesome road,
C   G
Going down that long lonesome road, Lord Lord
    D   G
And I ain't going to be treated this a-way.

LITTLE MAGGIE
(public domain)
KEY ON RECORD: B
CAPO: 4TH FRET

    G   F
Over yonder stands little Maggie
    G   D   G
With a dram glass in her hand
                 F
She's drinking away her troubles
    G   D   G
And courting some other man.

ALL THE GOOD TIMES ARE
PAST AND GONE
(public domain)
KEY ON RECORD: B
CAPO: 4TH FRET

G   C   G
I wish to the Lord I'd never been born
             D
Or died when I was young.
G   C   G
I never would have seen your sparkling blue eyes
    D   G
Or heard your lying tongue.
    [same chords for chorus]

ROLL ON BUDDY
(public domain)
KEY ON RECORD: B
CAPO: 4TH FRET

G
I'm going to that east pay road
   C   G
I'm going to that east pay road
   C   G
I'm going to the east I'm going to the west
        D   G
I'm going to the one that I love best
  [same chords for chorus]

SITTING ON TOP OF THE WORLD
(public domain)
KEY ON RECORD: C
CAPO: 5TH FRET

    G
Was in the Spring, one sunny day,
       C   G
My good gal left me, Lord she went away.

And now she's gone and I don't worry.
          D   G
Lord, I'm sitting on top of the world.

JESSE JAMES
(public domain)
KEY ON RECORD: C
CAPO: 5TH FRET

    G   C   G
Jesse James was a lad who killed many a man

He robbed the Glendale train.
    G   C   G
He stole from the rich and he gave to the poor
          D   G
With a hand and a heart and a brain.
         C   G
(chorus:) Jesse had a wife to mourn for his life,
         D
Three children they were brave.
              C   G
But that dirty little coward that shot Mr. Howard
       D   G
Has laid poor Jesse in his grave.

For all of these songs, the chords given here are for the key of G (except "Dark Hollow," for which the chords are in the key of D). On the recording, however, most of the songs are in keys other than G: A, B, and C. To play along with the recording, you can follow the chords as given, but to make the banjo sound in the right key, you will need a use a *capo*. A capo is a bar that can be strapped to the neck to shorten (and thus raise the pitch of) the strings. To play in A, put the capo on the second fret. For B, put it on the fourth fret. For C, it goes on the fifth. Since the capo does not touch the fifth string, the pitch of that string has to be raised separately, either by tightening the peg (though too much will break the string), or by use of a fifth string capo or small hooks in the neck to slip the string under. The pitch of the fifth string must be raised the same number of frets as the rest of the strings. Its pitch should match that of the first string fretted five frets up from the capo.

To play along with the recording, make sure the banjo is in tune using audio track 1, and place the capo at the right fret (with the fifth string tuned properly). Then, just by following the chords as though you were playing in G, you will be in the right key. Note: For "Dark Hollow," play the chords as given for the key of D, with the capo at the second fret. This will put you in the key of E, as on the recording.

Once you've learned how to use the capo and how to play the chords for the songs, try playing along with the recording. Keep a steady rhythm with any right-hand strum that feels natural—an up-and-down strum is fine for now. Once that comes easily, you're ready to try bluegrass style three-finger picking.

BLUEGRASS STYLE

For bluegrass picking you'll need metal finger picks for your index and middle fingers, plus a plastic thumb pick (you can find them in most music stores). When picking, place your ring and/or little finger firmly near the banjo's bridge.

The notation in this book is not standard music notation. It's called tablature, and here's how to read it: Each of the five lines represents a string (the top line is the first string, the bottom line is the fifth). The numbers on the lines indicate which fret of which string is being played by the left hand (0 means open string). An "x" on the first line means "rest"—leave a space the length of one note. The right-hand finger used to pick each note is shown directly below it: T means thumb, I means index, M means middle finger. Other symbols such as H, S, and P mean the note is created by something the left hand does: H means hammer-on, S means slide, P means pull-off, CH means choke. B means brush. (For more information on these techniques, check a banjo instruction book.) Under each measure there are two heavy horizontal lines (three in "All the Good Times Are Past and Gone," which is in 3/4 time). These mark off the beats. As you can see, there is space for four notes in each beat of up-tempo bluegrass time, and two beats in each measure.

To get your right hand used to what it has to do, start by practicing these three right-hand rolls (picking patterns):

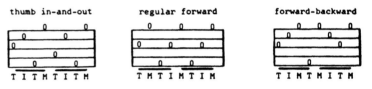

The thumb in-and-out roll is good to start with to develop your sense of time. In this roll, the thumb plays the two "inside" (non-fifth string) notes exactly on the two beats in a standard measure of bluegrass time.

Example:

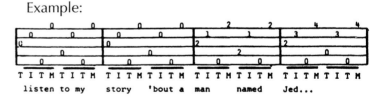

So if you play this roll along with "The Ballad of Jed Clampett" or any other up-tempo bluegrass song, your thumb will be hitting the third and fourth strings alternately just as the bass and guitar play their accented bass notes. Try playing the roll smoothly in time with some of the songs. "Mountain Dew" and "It's in My Mind to Ramble" are two of the slower cuts, but you can adjust the speed of any of the faster songs using the *PlayBack+* feature online so that they are slow enough to play along with. Once you can play along smoothly using the thumb in-and-out roll, try the same thing with each of the other two rolls. These rolls both accent the first note, so make sure that note comes right on the first (usually the strongest) beat of each measure.

Once you're comfortable with these basic rolls, you're probably ready to try picking a little melody. Start by working out the first part of "Dueling Banjos," by ear or by using the tablature presented later in this book. It's slow and not difficult, especially if you use one finger to barre all the strings across the fifth fret on the C chord and across the seventh fret on the D chord. The first part of "Dueling Banjos" doesn't use a bluegrass roll, but it will help you acquaint yourself with playing melodies on the banjo.

The next step is to work out some of the tablature in this book. All of the breaks (solos) written out are of about the same level of difficulty. Just pick one you'd like to learn and work it out, a measure or two at a time. To help you learn the break and to check whether it sounds right, listen to the recording. *The banjo notation in this book is taken directly from the banjo breaks on the recordings.* As with learning to play the beginning rolls, it will probably be quite helpful to slow down the audio. It may also help to raise the banjo's volume over the rest of the band by moving the balance button.

Working out breaks is one point where you may find the going a bit rough, but keep at it and, in time, you will succeed. If you think you need more detailed instruction, you may try working with a teacher. Work toward playing smoothly, right in time with the banjo on the recording, even if it means playing the recording slower. Once you can play breaks up to speed with the recording, you can certainly consider yourself a competent bluegrass banjo player, ready to play with a band (and not just a pre-recorded one!).

BACKUP

The play-along recordings will give you a good chance to practice a very important part of your playing: backup. By playing not only breaks, but backup behind the rest of the music, you will have a chance to practice the techniques expected of a banjo player in a bluegrass band: fill in licks, "chopping" (also known as "choonking"—picking chords crisply on the offbeats), and smooth rolls to keep the sound flowing. Listen carefully to what the banjo on the recording does: how it plays along differently behind the mandolin or the guitar than it does behind the fiddle or vocals, how its loudness varies depending on what contributes best to the overall band sound.

Most of the actual techniques used in backing up are not very different from what you use for solos, but you should learn them and learn them well. There is a big difference between good and mediocre banjo backup—it affects the way the whole band sounds. To do the job right doesn't depend on being fancy. It's much more important to keep a steady rhythm and to play with sensitivity to the overall sound of the band. To develop these traits, practice, practice, practice!

The Ballad of Jed Clampett

This is the opening break (count: 1 2 3 4, 1 2 3). Banjo also takes third and fourth (final) breaks.

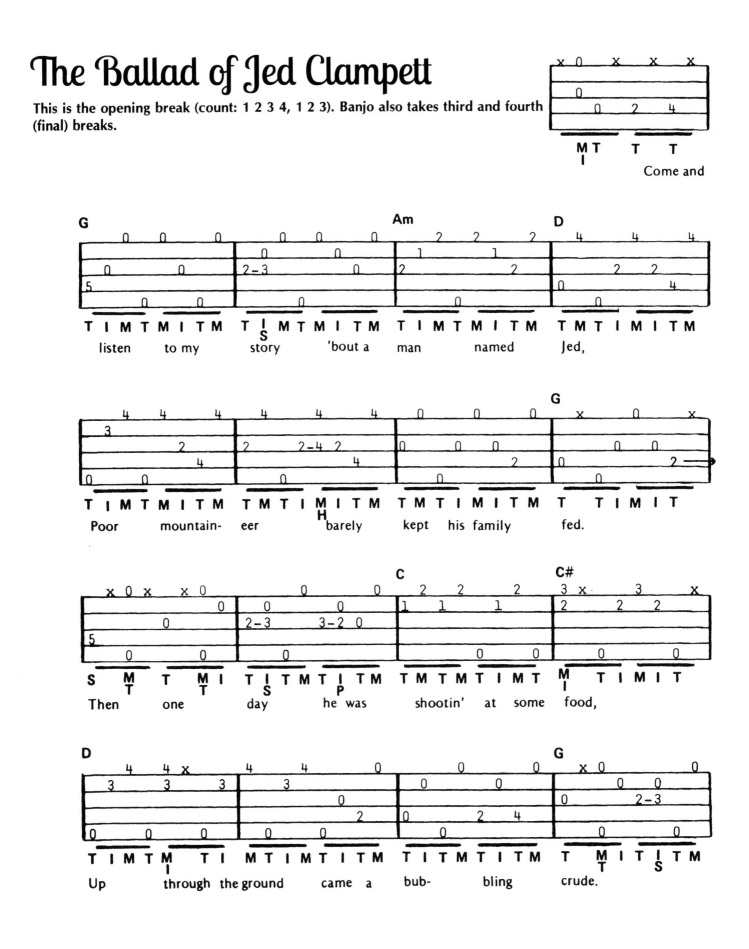

Foggy Mountain Breakdown

This is the opening chorus (count: 1 2 3 4, 1 2 3). Banjo also plays next two choruses. After two fiddle choruses, banjo plays two more, guitar plays two, and banjo finishes with two and a "shave and a haircut" ending.

It's in My Mind to Ramble

(Opening count: 1 2 3). Banjo takes second break.

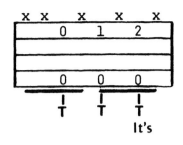

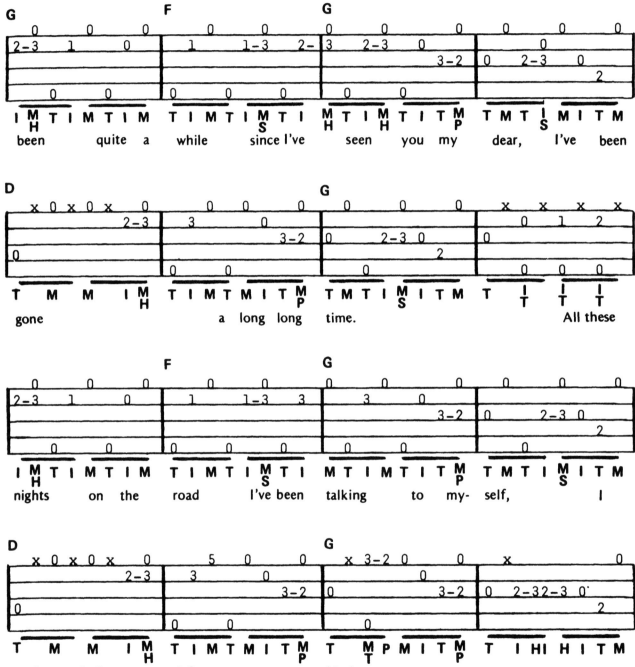

Salty Dog Blues

This is the opening break (count: 1 2 3). Banjo also takes fourth break.

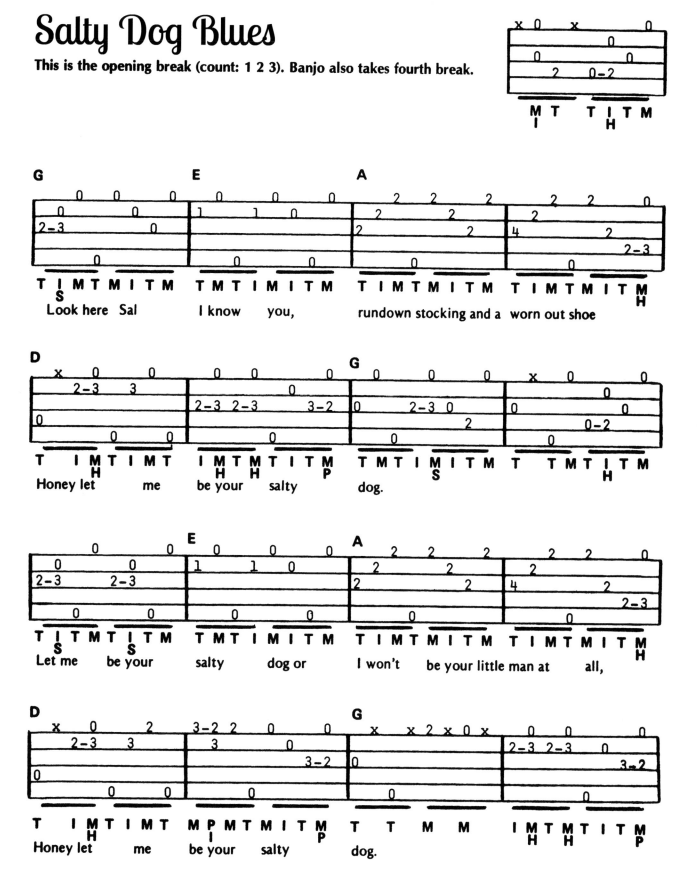

Late Last Night

(Opening count: 1 2 3). Banjo takes third break.

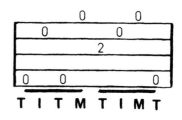

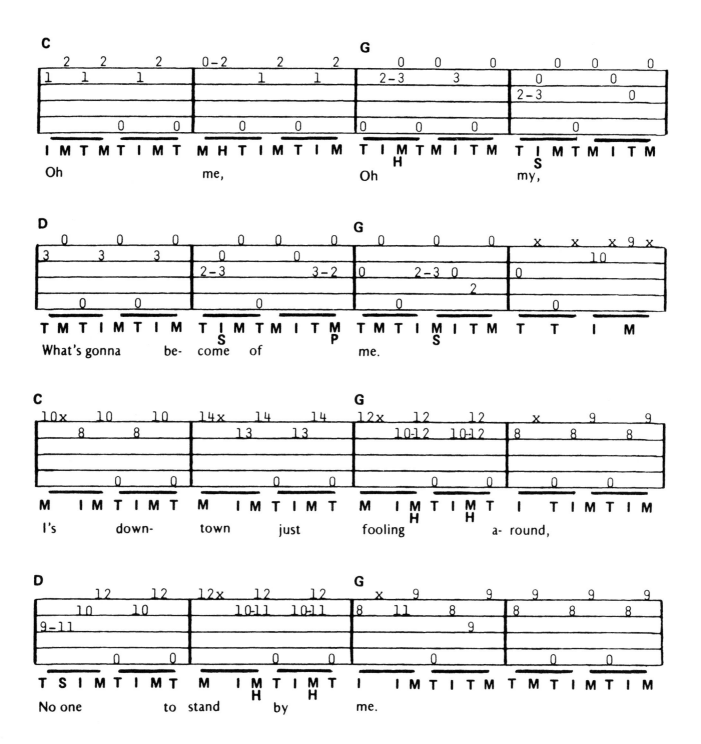

Dueling Banjos

This is the first half of the arrangement on the recording (count: 1 2 3 4). The second half is very similar, but all up-tempo.

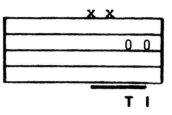

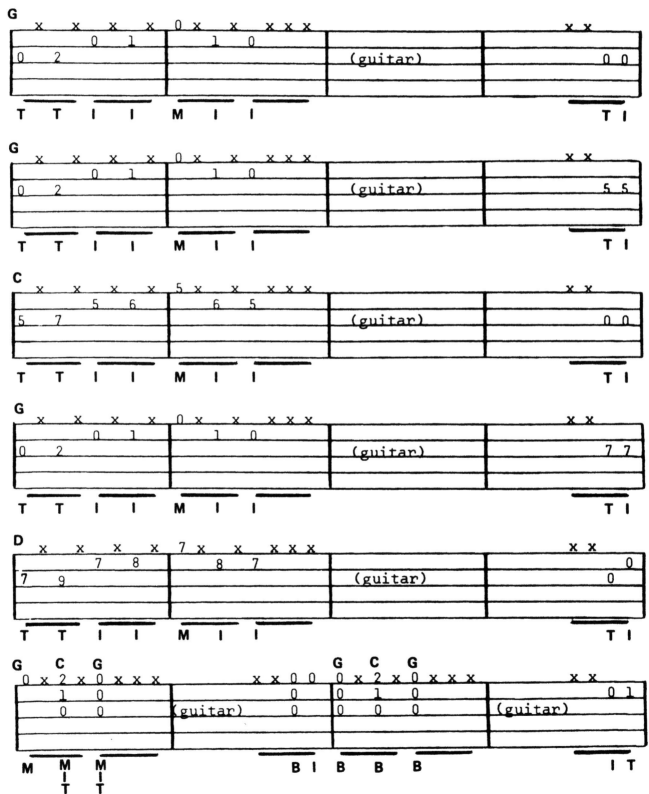

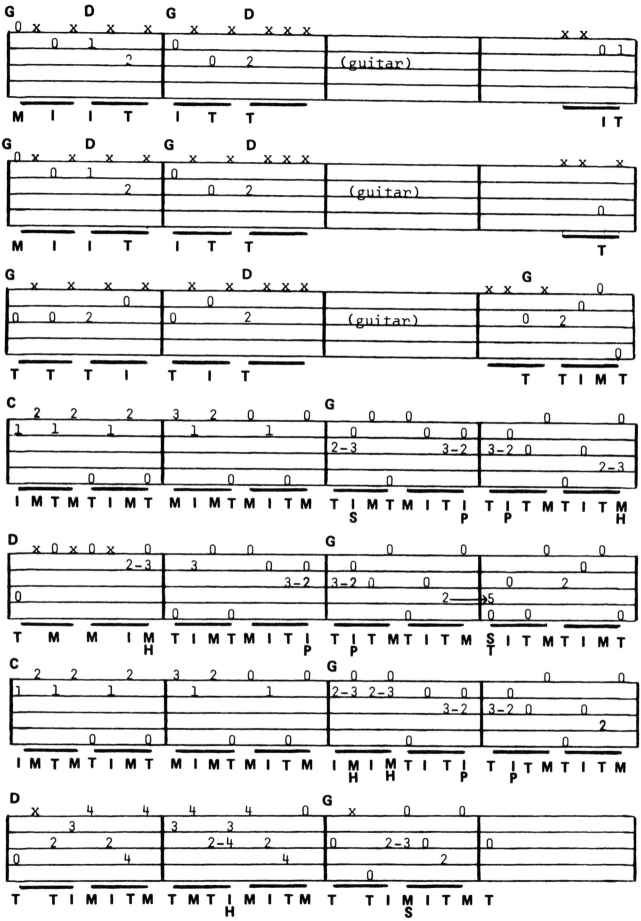

Mountain Dew

(Opening count: 1 2, 1 2). Banjo takes third break.

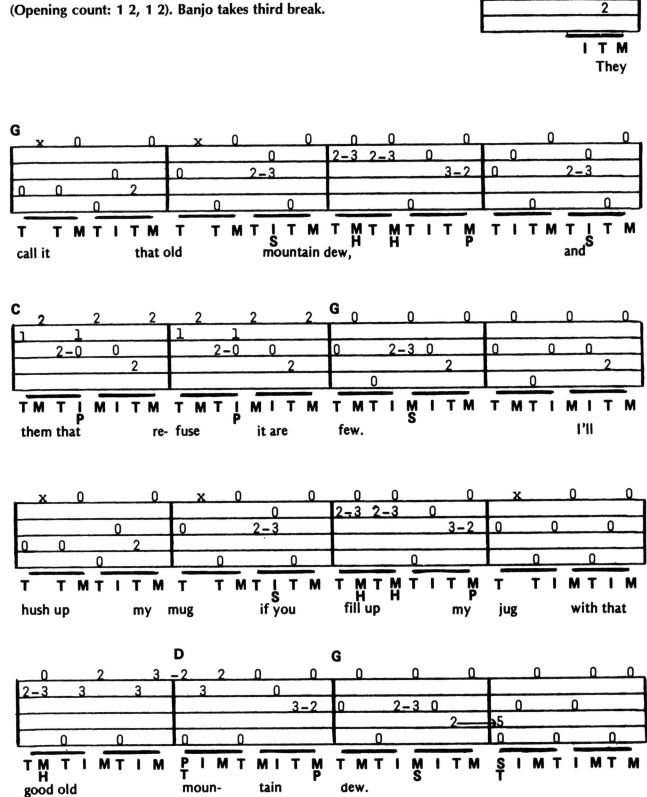

Lonesome Road Blues

Banjo takes opening break (count: 1 2 3 4, 1 2 3).

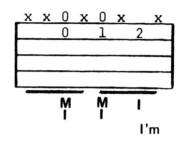

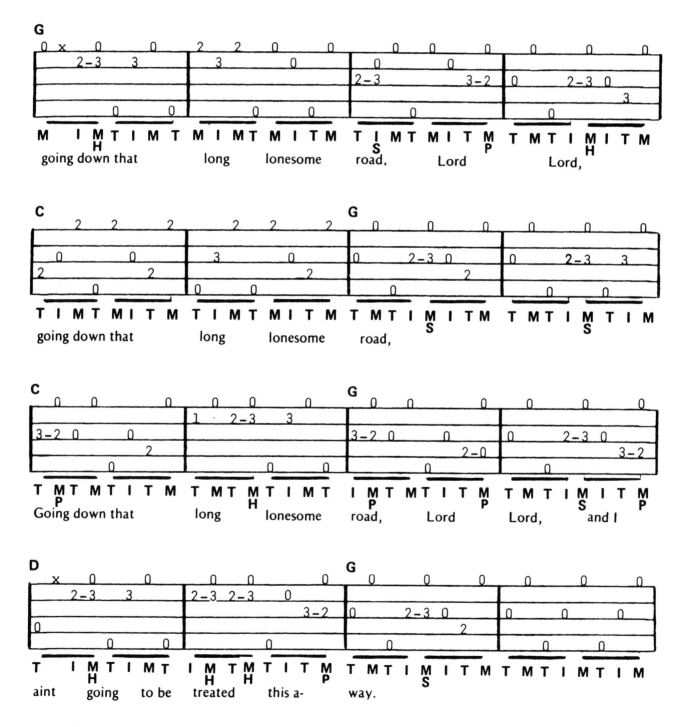

Little Maggie

This is the opening break (count: 1 2, 1 2). Banjo also takes fourth break.

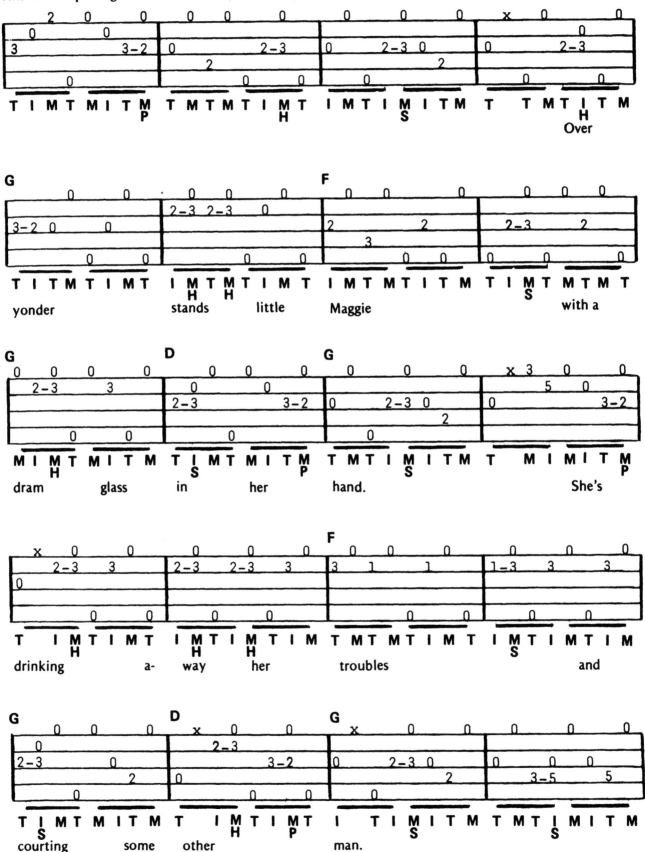

All the Good Times Are Past and Gone

(Opening count: 1 2 3, 1). Banjo takes second break.

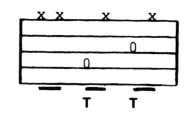

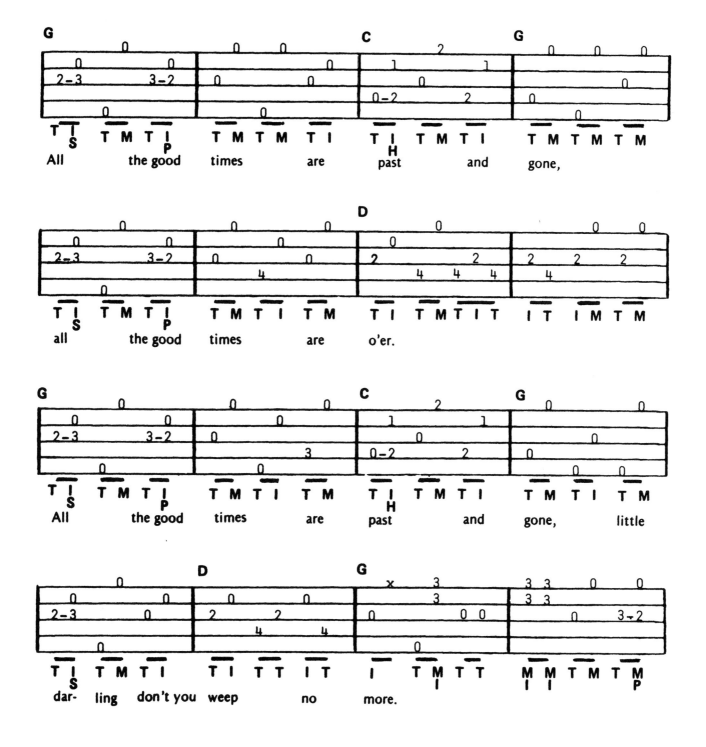

Roll on Buddy

(Opening count: 1 2 3). Banjo takes second break.

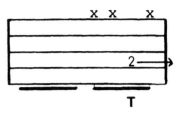

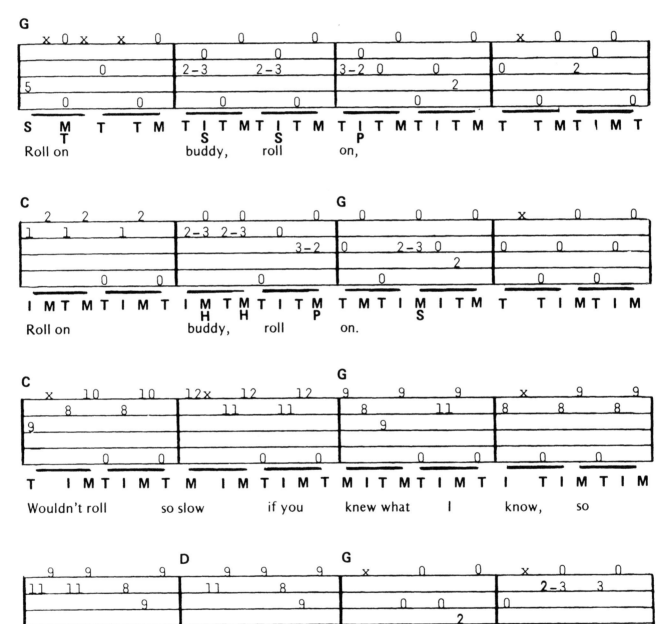

Sitting on Top of the World

Banjo takes opening break (count: 1 2 3 4, 1 2 3).

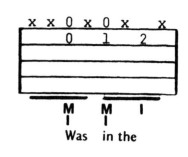

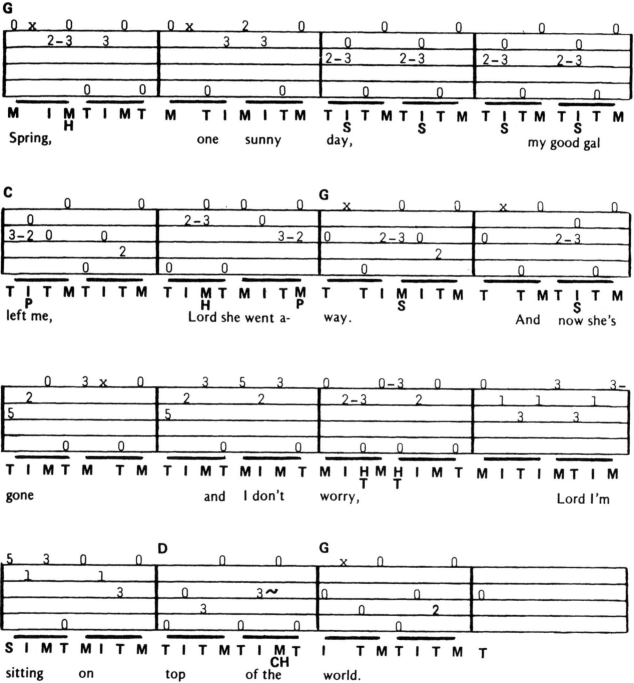

Jesse James

Banjo takes opening break (count: 1 2 3).

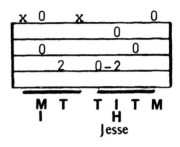

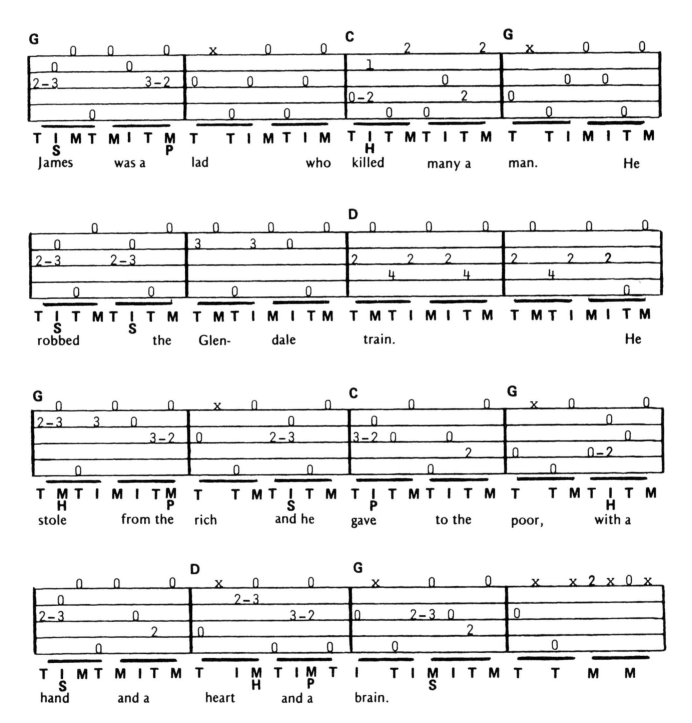

PETE WERNICK

a/k/a "Dr. Banjo," is known for his many roles—and rolls (banjo rolls, that is)—in bluegrass music: the hot-picking force behind the award-winning Hot Rize and Country Cooking bands, best-selling author and video instructor, songwriter, and President of the International Bluegrass Music Association.

Pete's books and videos have sold over a quarter million copies, and include *Beginning Bluegrass Banjo, Branching Out on the Banjo*, and *How to Make a Band Work*. His week-long banjo camps in Colorado and traveling clinics have helped and inspired players worldwide.

Pete took up banjo as a teenager in his native New York City, closely studying Earl Scruggs records. While completing B.A. and doctorate sociology degrees at Columbia, he played in local bands and found time to host a bluegrass radio program. While a sociologist at Cornell in upstate New York, he formed Country Cooking whose innovative recordings in 1971–75 are still among Round Records' top releases.

In 1976 Pete moved to Colorado where he recorded the solo *Dr. Bango Steps Out* (Flying Fish). After collaborating on the album, Pete and Tim O' Brien started the Hot Rize band in 1978. Going full tilt until 1990, the foursome was a major attraction and creative force in bluegrass, respected for both dynamic stage shows and finely crafted recordings (Sugar Hill and Flying Fish). The group scored repeated #1 hits on the bluegrass chart, including the Wernick-penned "Just Like You." Hot Rize also received IBMA's coveted Entertainer of the Year award and a Grammy® nomination. Pete is associated with Waldo Otto, the daffy steel guitar player of Hot Rize's beloved alter-egos, Red Knuckles and the Trailblazers.

Pete's current performance schedule includes festivals and appearances with his new "virtual bluegrass" group, The Live Five, and with his singer/guitarist wife Joan as a duet (Dr. and Nurse Banjo). His solo album *On a Roll* (Sugar Hill), including both bluegrass and The Live Five, rode the national chart for over a year, with another #1 single, "Ruthie."

COUNTRY COOKING

specialized in modern as well as traditional bluegrass and were together for about ten years. During this time they recorded two albums on Rounder Records, and provided backup for mandolin player Frank Wakefield on a third.

On this album, in order to help musicians to develop basic bluegrass techniques, they stick mostly to traditional bluegrass, based on the styles of groups such as Bill Monroe and the Blue Grass Boys, Flatt and Scruggs and the Foggy Mountain Boys, and the Stanley Brothers and the Clinch Mountain Boys.

Hal Leonard Banjo Play-Along Series

BANJO PLAY-ALONG

AUDIO
ACCESS
INCLUDED

INCLUDES TAB

*The Banjo Play-Along Series will help you play your favorite songs quickly and easily with incredible backing tracks to help you sound like a bona fide pro! Just follow the banjo tab, listen to the demo track on the CD or online audio to hear how the banjo should sound, and then play along with the separate backing tracks. The CD is playable on any CD player and also is enhanced so Mac and PC users can adjust the recording to any tempo without changing the pitch! Books with online audio also include **PLAYBACK+** options such as looping and tempo adjustments. Each Banjo Play-Along pack features eight cream of the crop songs.*

1. BLUEGRASS
Ashland Breakdown • Deputy Dalton • Dixie Breakdown • Hickory Hollow • I Wish You Knew • I Wonder Where You Are Tonight • Love and Wealth • Salt Creek.
00102585 Book/CD Pack.........................$14.99

2. COUNTRY
East Bound and Down • Flowers on the Wall • Gentle on My Mind • Highway 40 Blues • If You've Got the Money (I've Got the Time) • Just Because • Take It Easy • You Are My Sunshine.
00105278 Book/CD Pack.........................$14.99

3. FOLK/ROCK HITS
Ain't It Enough • The Cave • Forget the Flowers • Ho Hey • Little Lion Man • Live and Die • Switzerland • Wagon Wheel.
00119867 Book/CD Pack.........................$14.99

4. OLD-TIME CHRISTMAS
Away in a Manger • Hark! the Herald Angels Sing • Jingle Bells • Joy to the World • O Holy Night • O Little Town of Bethlehem • Silent Night • We Wish You a Merry Christmas.
00119889 Book/CD Pack.........................$14.99

5. PETE SEEGER
Blue Skies • Get up and Go • If I Had a Hammer (The Hammer Song) • Kisses Sweeter Than Wine • Mbube (Wimoweh) • Sailing Down My Golden River • Turn! Turn! Turn! (To Everything There Is a Season) • We Shall Overcome.
00129699 Book/CD Pack.........................$17.99

6. SONGS FOR BEGINNERS
Bill Cheatham • Black Mountain Rag • Cripple Creek • Grandfather's Clock • John Hardy • Nine Pound Hammer • Old Joe Clark • Will the Circle Be Unbroken.
00139751 Book/CD Pack.........................$14.99

7. BLUEGRASS GOSPEL
Cryin' Holy unto the Lord • How Great Thou Art • I Saw the Light • I'll Fly Away • I'll Have a New Life • Man in the Middle • Turn Your Radio On • Wicked Path of Sin.
00147594 Book/Online Audio $14.99

8. CELTIC BLUEGRASS
Billy in the Low Ground • Cluck Old Hen • Devil's Dream • Fisher's Hornpipe • Little Maggie • Over the Waterfall • The Red Haired Boy • Soldier's Joy.
00160077 Book/Online Audio $14.99

HAL•LEONARD®
www.halleonard.com